Hiraeth

Hiraeth

FIRST EDITION

ISBN: 9798522123383

Edited by Vanessa Dremé.

You become more dangerous when you learn to
control the demons within you...

For peace of mind, I had to learn to disregard blood...

Dedicated to an actress that inspired a lot of these poems. We haven't met but I hope we do. The last poem is mainly for her. Yes, her existence inspired a lot of these poems some point after 23.

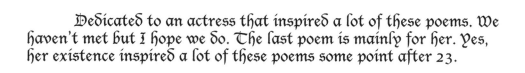

EVERY 'you' IS FOR HER AND EVERY **'you'** IS FOR GOD. I DON'T WANT TO DISCLOSE WHO THE OTHER 'you's ARE FOR.

1.

Where you're considered as less than nothing,
It's not called home.
Where you're not seen as an equal,
It's not called society.
Where you're seen as a slave,
It's not called freedom.
Where you're truly valued,
It's a place that seems to have never even existed.

You blurred my visions
And expected me to make life changing decisions.
You were once the angels in my mind
Now, you're the demons on my shoulder.
I was wrong to let my guard down and be blind.
Let it be known,
My heart has never been colder.
Can I ask you what you get out of it?

You clearly made me the misfit.
You made sure I was brought up like an orphan,
Like the prodigal son.
How can I be so much
Yet, less than nothing?
All you did was make me run
From the reality as well as the fantasy.
You expect things to be fine
While sugarcoating it all
But I always preferred the bitter.
I'm not here to watch you gloat.
You can't fake a feeling of ecstasy.

You say it's an addiction and an escape,
But why does it feel like a safe haven?
Why does it feel like I'm better off with it
Than I am around you?
You say it's my worst addiction,

But why does it feel like a remedy?
Why does it feel like the only suitable solution?

You say it's bondage,
But why does it give me a sense of belonging?
Why does it make me feel like I'm finally capable
Of forgetting my lost wings
And falling in love with being the wolf I've become?
Yet through all this I see a sliver of hope
Just enough for the others.
So, I write it for you.

2.

The reason I can't sleep at night
Is 'cause the demons in me come out
When there is no light.
They sit down,
Trying to bring out the darkness deep inside,
Claiming it's an essential aura of mine.
When even they fear the damn beast inside me.
Even they don't know how to stay inside a line.
They want the example set free.
I don't try to get rid of them
Because they make sure everyone that loves…leaves.

So, they can condemn…
Yet it's something each one achieves.
They'll stay here till they're driven
Away by madness or fear,
Where they end up getting crazier
The longer they linger around me.
See, once the beast is out, nothing will be clear.
Even redemption will be something
You won't dare to see.

They cause the pain in my heart
But even they don't know it fell apart.
Broken time after time,
Love is just a curse.
I know I don't need it or deserve it.
It does more destruction than the Devil.

You say you can't come down to my level.
Stay where you are,
I can smell you're not built for this.
You think you're holy
By hitting me with verse after verse.

I'm just trying to tell you
That I'm forever meant to enjoy the company

Of the demons who fear but taunt the beast.
When I'm done, they know I'm exhausted
So, they decide to walk away.
All I see are the traces of darkness
That glows in their eyes.

3.

Usually you're in my head,
Like the bitter part of my subconscious.
I don't even get to sleep in my own bed,
I don't even think God could give me
A hint on how to be cautious.

All you want me to do is make sure of one thing:
The destruction of my closest circle.
Through me, you want to cause a mess.
The fact I get to see you should be a gift
But in every way, it's causing a rift.
I don't think I have enough finesse.
You've made movement in my life sedated.

I was wrong enough to make a deal
Just to make sure I feel.
I feel like I'm stuck with all of you,
For you cling onto any part of me you can.
Nothing you say is even true,
But you shatter all my hope.

They say a lot about man.
You have made me
What everyone warned me about,
I don't even have a proper way to cope.
All you did was protect the seed,
Guaranteeing evil would sprout.
I feel like I'm beyond being fixed and saved.
All I can guess is that you want it that way
And Lord do I try to pray.

I think you've become a part of me,
But something I will have to leave,
To have a trick up my sleeve.
I'm tired of bleeding down each knee.

4.

Shattered glass,
Let this dreaded time pass.
It isn't just you,
It's with everyone in the crew.
I put up walls for everyone,
Otherwise, I'll just run.
There is no hands-on deck.

All because of a label,
Some even think of it as a fable.
As it sits beside the title damaged
Yet another epithet I salvaged-
Unlovable.

Like broken shards of a mirror,
Fractured hearts are no longer clearer.
Some say they see pain,
Like I want to get rid of my brain.
Some say they see rage,
When they are the ones
That rattle the beast's cage.

Some say they see someone lost,
Like my heart got caught in the frost.
Some say they see a reflection.
They hardly realize they look at a puddle of water
Rather than the entire ocean.

Where there is never going to be
A sailor who can guide another through,
They'll bid me adieu.
As they pass through treacherous waters,
Where nothing can be predicted
But a torn piece of art hardly depicted,
Only felt or revealed
And so rarely appealed.

These waters are dark.
You never know what lurks beneath you.
In the bottom lies the spark
Where the only protected ones
Are the special selected few.
When the storm starts,
You never know when it will settle,
Until you see a black rose petal-
The smallest symbol of mercy,
As well as my parting gift as a courtesy.

Beware all those who believe they can swim…
This darkness can tear your soul apart, limb by limb.
Beware of all those who believe lies will save them.
It will shine within them like a gem
And the darkness will devour it.
You will find yourself falling in an endless pit.
How can I warn you of what's to come?
It isn't a risk for some.

5.

You say you relate to me,
You say you see a bit of yourself in me,
You say you see a reflection.
Hell, I'm born out of a messed-up complexion.
But most of all, what do you see yourself in?
My soul is in pieces.
Which shard do you relate to or care for?
Never say you feel a connection.
It's just better that way for your protection.

You will never have the capacity to handle more
From me and my thoughts.
I can't wait for the day it rots.
At least I'll have stopped thinking,
Cause I do it so much even as I'm blinking,
I want every link to break,
Till I'm freed of my demons
To ensure no harm to others but myself.

See, I am my own demon.
So, freedom will only weaken
But I'm praying that
That weakness will be a beacon
And I pray further that you realize
This sacrifice was for you.

What else can I do?
I haven't exactly been raised like you
And just like everyone else, I'm different.
Misunderstood more than related to,
You can't even see through
So, you back off,
Like I've got some contagious cough.

If there's something wrong with me,
How do I tell if it's spiritual or psychological?
'Cause neither one has an answer for me.

Both just leave me be.

I'd love to say it happens to the best of us
But I'm not exactly the best.
I'm more of a wild thing,
One you'd like to keep away from the rest.

6.

There is no us
So, I guess there is no fuss.
What you feel or relate to,
I'm praying you get out of it.
I don't know what you make out of this.
Unfortunately, the world doesn't offer a quick fix.

Misconception and me
Along with so much more, we're closely knit
And blame doesn't even solve
Anything closely related.
It just adds more to my burdens
Than the ones I already have.
I feel like there's a part of me
Long gone and belated.

There is a piece of me that resides with you
And I can't think of a safer place,
For when I hold a funeral
For the person I used to be.
Unsaid words
With thoughts not acted upon,
They will be the mark of my gravestone.

I will take a moment of peace
Before I breathe my last.
As the person you used to know,
Before I set myself on this new path,
Wishing it never came to this.

7.

Bound to burn
Bound to learn
Bound to turn
Bound by the dark
Bound by everyone who set the mark
Bound by anyone who sees a spark
Bound to those who tried to give me a head start
Bound to never have a heart
Bound to always only be set apart.

I am what you made me
Not what I decided I want to be.
You turned me into a beast,
While you all enjoyed your feast.
Incapable to love or be loved,
The resentment was shoved,
The hate was fostered
And for a moment you prospered,
The disownment was harvested
And I became the bad seed,
Even though it was made sure to your misdeed.

Sold my soul to the Devil,
Ended up being called the rebel.
Also, a never-to-return prodigal,
They call me episodical.
Is it really my fault I feel too much?
My soul really needs a crutch.
Is it really my fault I hurt too much?

All I get told is "life is such".
I'm bleeding on others.
God knows how many tried to be mothers
And you made me think I'm really a burden.
I'm not something you hide behind a curtain.
Call me rotten
Call me alone

Call me dark
Call me the worst influence.
There's nothing you can condone.
For you were the one that snuffed out my spark.

8.

I try my best to see
I try my best to be
I try my best to feel
I try my best to heal.
I tried my best just to make you smile
But your reaction made it vile.
I tried my best to give you my all
And you stood there,
As you watched me fall.

But I belong here,
I don't live in fear
Down here it's dark
And I'm the only spark.
Watch the death glow in my eyes
As you feel the fear in you rise.

That ephemeral moment where I was good,
When I was kind
When I was an ideal.
It didn't even let me heal
It had people blind,
Convincing me that I could
And when I fell back
No one wanted to catch me.

So, the darkness made me free.
I got scars I could live with.
A small price for endless bliss
And it wasn't a myth
I hardly ever reminisce.
My scars became my throne,
Closest to my heart as they are shown.

And there were times
I really needed to feel the pain,
To feel the tears, pour out like rain.

No matter how dreadful the storm,
It never showed in any form
That's when I felt all the harm.
I could ever do to others
And not even one knew out of all my brothers.

They formed a part of me,
As they were placed in front of my heart,
In front of the door of my dark soul to be
And it tore me apart.

9.

I'm not allowed to speak
Because I'm a freak,
An outcast,
The black sheep,
You believe I'm darker than the Devil
And I am
Nowhere close to giving a damn.

There is nothing left to settle.
That's why I don't weep.
I just want this life to end fast.
Take me to where you are, Dad,
For keeping up with the pretense of being bad
Only exhausts me.

I'm too kind for this world,
My emotions left preserved,
My behavior left observed.
This world does more harm than good
And I end up doing more than I should.
This world leaves people damaged
This world leaves people in pain
This world leaves people broken.

Some people think they have everything managed
But it's a cycle and chain.
You get hurt the very second you let your soul open,
Some think it's all in the mind
But we don't feel everything with our brain.
Is it better to remain confined,
Or better to find?
Find a way out of all this pain.

10.

You really have to get out of your shell.
I noticed that when I fell,
Fell so hard for you,
And you didn't even give me a clue
That would show me you died inside,
Becoming someone completely new
And letting the rest hide.

I write about you for it is the only way
I can truly still be with you.
Although my emotions want to bid you adieu,
In my head and in my heart,
Even though they're far apart,
And deep within I knew,
You were just too good to be true.

I write about you.
It is the only sane way to pass my time
While I lie in wait.
You tossed me away like a dime
But I still decide not to turn to hate.

You got tired of the chase.
So, you decided to change your phase.
The hell in me and
The heaven in you
Opposed each other to a catastrophic level
And when you saw the Devil,
You told me that your love wasn't true.
So, just like the rest you decided to flee.

Take me to court,
Send me to the moon,
Confide in your fort,
You'll feel things happening soon.
You'd do me a favor

And feel a little safer
Maybe even braver.

Don't forget, a wolf never gets tamed.
I don't mind being blamed.
I can only be silenced
But how long will it last?
I'll make up for everything lost quite fast
And things will be balanced.

I'm searching for you
But the emptiness in me,
Devours everyone else.
Can you dream up a version of us
Where my heart isn't black and blue?
Can you dream up a version of us
Where I'm not one of the rebels?

You left me at port
Just like everyone else in my life.
I have dismal emotions of sort,
I had no idea my heart
Was being held onto by a knife.
You had me under a false impression
That I was in paradise.
It was a brutal illusion to recognize.

Take me to the middle of the night,
Where I can try my best to make it all right.
I promise that the wolf won't bite.
I'll try to be a knight.
I wake up and find myself nowhere close
With a dead rose.
It was just another transient bliss
At the bottom of an abyss.

11.

I see it in the distance.
As I sit here on the edge,
I look down only to see
That some things are afar and some are close.
There is no controlling it
There is no leaping forward
There is no skipping ahead
There is no sugarcoating it.
Numbing it away would be cowardice:
'You have to ride through it.'

Then I fall,
It seems endless,
This wasn't the edge of a cliff.
No, this here was a dark abyss and
It seems as if I pushed myself over.

It gets darker
To a point where,
A few meters above seemed to be lighter.
At this point, I'm alone.
This is the way it has to be.
This is how it was always meant to be.
Deep inside I know that
Yet, still I wish someone was here.

The darkness isn't just around me,
It's inside me.
It snuffed out the light inside
before I even knew I would be here.

12.

I don't see fire,
I don't see blood,
Maybe this might be
A hell of my making.
Maybe this is just punishment
From heaven above,
Maybe this is me
Becoming a grim reaper.

It seems as if this fall
May come to an abrupt end
But when all is said and done,
I will have changed.
I see my scars open.
They don't turn to the wounds they once were.
The fur comes out
And my skin rips further.

I realize that I am transforming
To the very thing I loved but suppressed.
The wolf wants to take over.
There is no fighting it now,
I also know there will be no coming back
For the bridges that I burned
Are only drifting farther.
There won't be any water in between,
Galaxies will fill in the gaps,
Ensuring I won't have anything to go back to.

My jaw burns
As I feel the fangs come out,
My head is throbbing
As my eyes change color.

I see the faint glow
Of the bloody red eyes.
I know I won't see things the same way,

My judgment will be clearer
It will be more primal
It will come from my gut in moments,
I'll bite more,
I will be sinking my teeth into flesh.

There will be no speaking to people
Who won't understand.
There will be no barking,
Only howling to the moon
To the one who knows I am
Who I truly was all along.

13.
(Part 2 of 12.)

I see my hands turn to paws,
My nails turn to talons.
Things I touch will tear.
I grow bigger
As my bones change form,
I know I will be faster
But not fast enough to escape the darkness.

I know there's more coming
For some of my wounds stay
Open and bleeding.
I look like I walked out of a nightmare.
I look like I am here to bring many to the people.

Suddenly, I feel the ground
Beneath my paws.
I snarl loud enough
To warn the people in the distance,
I can smell their fear.
I know what I am here to do,
There is no evading it.
My very will brought me here.

I run in the moonlight, through the forest.
I growl along the way,
I hear villages tremble as I pass by.
I know I will have to learn to adapt.
Adapt to being feared,
Adapt to being hated,
Adapt to being a target,
Adapt to being blamed.

I shall wear this pride
As I learn to own what I am now.
Who I was inside
Has finally been unleashed,

There will be more to come,
There will be bloodshed,
There will be fear to feed off of
And it will only grow.

I see a halo,
A crown
Of fire on my head.
I'm the wolf of hell
Here to ensure misery.
I know I am here on my terms.
So, the demons know to stay in line.
I can harm even them,
They know I am above them.
All they can do is taunt me behind my back.

14.

The damage has been done.
The wounds you'd expect to see
Are no longer there,
Don't think I've run.
I'm at a place only the Devil knows where,
Don't expect things to fix-
You damn well knew the risk.

I never lied about myself.
It was as clear as the label
Of a book on a shelf,
I didn't lose anything.
You, the Devil and me would make three
But my duo with the Devil
Is exactly what keeps me free.

I tried to give you a place by my side
But you weren't in it for the long ride.
I put my hand out
And I didn't want to stand out.
You kept running in circles
And I had no intention of being in the middle.
I live off such goddamn chains,
You can't bind me, tie me,
Lock me or limit me.

Which is why I look to the moon.
She watches over me as I run
In the wild as the darkness takes over.
I now realize I want someone
Wild enough to run with me too,
To explore the beauty of the night,
To encounter things in each other's company,
To howl together.

And as we let a piece of our souls
Out in those memories,

You look back at them
Only when you revisit,
Realizing you only collected a part of my soul.
I can't take back what I've given
And that part was only meant
To be given to you,
Like the shedding of fur.

15.

Remember that as I now stroll down
These streets of hell,
Where the demons won't let you
Catch a glimpse of me.
I won't be able to shelter you here,
The Devil collects his due,
Which is why I let go of my hold on you.

He whispered in my ear,
"Don't worry, she isn't going to stick around either."
And I made sure of it.
The wolf of hell has his own duty.
I'm not a guard dog.
I ensure justice of sins.

So, if you haven't committed any,
I suggest you go back
To wherever you came from.
I tend to feed on the innocents.
Here I am respected.
If I give a glimpse of my fangs,
Even the demons have a rush of fear.

You were lucky I knew you
Through the ones that once meant something.
You lied
And I hadn't really died.
I never wanted you to be my bride
The way they wanted.
You only readjusted my focus
On the moon however distant she may be.

This crown on my head,
Forged by the founding flames of Hell,
It knows no heir.
Nor can it be made for a queen,
I rule alone.

For it is forever.

I can't play little games
Not when I talk with the very one
Who created them.

16.

A promise to be there always, is twisted.
Only one of us believes in loyalty,
Only one of us sees reality in its hideous form,
While the other one sugarcoats to live by it.
I never lied to you
But your very words opposed your actions
And I couldn't fall down that spiral.

This darkness consumes me but at least
It guides me away from negativity like you.
Even if it is just to protect his investment,
At least he watches my back
From the knives you want to stab in it.
You threw the word family
Yet you know nothing of it.

You raised the topic
As a plea to use my fear,
You thought it was a weakness
But you didn't realize it's my very strength.
I believe in loyalty
Even if I may be a member of Hell,
But the foundation of my throne
Is built on strong values that stood still
Through constant pressure.

You built your foundation on lies,
I would have tried to catch you as you fell,
Before your foundation
Collapsed from beneath you,
Only to have you buried underneath.

You only failed to understand
That I hadn't talked of myself
The way you did.
You'd let such positive words flourish about me
And there I'd be to deny them.

I warned you not to have such high expectations.
You refused me so I had to stand by
And watch in the darkness.

You never understood that this darkness
Is precisely what formed me.
You told me it was a phase
Not ready to listen as I explained.
You thought you knew.
You thought your age made you mature
But human concepts of time can't be tied to
Non-human concepts of damage.

I never hid my scars,
Your ignorance pushed me farther.
I told them I couldn't think
Through your perspective.
The one thing I lacked in a grave manner,
I told them that neither would they,
Nor would you ever understand mine,
Because I don't hide it.
Yet you're too blinded to even see it.
It's even the core of my humor
Which you appreciated at first,
But didn't you stop to think
About why I told you
I am not just a human-
I'm part Satan too.

And we all know that girls
Can't outlive the Devil.
They are attracted at first
Then they grow up to realize it's about self-respect.
While I sit here and own it
At least he saw my worth.

17.

They told me to keep moving forward
That I was heading the right way,
I knew this journey wasn't going to
Involve the others.
Now they can barely stand the sight of me,
Yet I don't remember
That part of the arrangement.

They never said I'd turn into this,
Yet they are free of blame.
Who are they to see into my future?
They barely knew who I used to be,
I'm the whisper ghosts barely hear.
A name that the demons dare to speak,
The people beg mercy of me.

I became more like the wind,
In and out before people realized
My absence left a dent in society.
I walked out and stayed out.
I watched as they squandered.
I knew my existence was beyond such things.

I was cursed with seeing things differently.
I was cursed to have a head
That takes on too much at a time.
I saw seven moves ahead
While people were left wondering
About the one I made way back when.

When I had nothing but myself,
When I still saw everyone
For who they truly were,
It disgusted me.
Forcing me to push myself away.

18.

I am too cold for most,
The rest believe, I'm hotter
Than a scorching sun.
Either way, no one can keep me around,
My moves can't be predicted.
My mind is homicidal,
Taught to kill the very life and will of anyone.

They seem to think they win
When I walk out.
At first it seems great
But a seed remains.
It creeps up slowly,
Growing like a cancer,
Undetected yet vicious.

I wish I could say that I didn't choose this
But this failsafe keeps me whole.
It gives me purpose…
At least I know it'll last.
What I have chosen to forsake is nothing
Compared to what it has to offer me.
It's all on my terms.

As memories come back,
I hardly believe the person I used to be.
I'm thankful they don't flood my mind.
As they rage into the heart,
Memories are dangerous,
They bring back emotions
Like a strong fragrance
And when they do,
Emotions seep into your bones.

You don't ever just shake that off.
If I were to return to
My younger self with all I have now,

I would never be the same as I was.
Maybe it was for the best.
You once said that I should prove everyone wrong,
When they think I am not capable.
You pulled me forward
So, here I sit on my throne
Ahead of all of them.

With the foundation so strong,
Created by the scars of the past,
The flames of hell forged it.
I look down onto those who beg for mercy.
They were the ones
Who had once neglected me.

Here I sit as I see their regret,
I held on to what you said.
You may have forgotten me,
Yet here I stand, ready to lean on it.
For I know it was fostered
From honesty at some point.

If it hadn't come from you,
I wouldn't have landed up here.
I have an empire,
I have a crown,
I have a throne.
Everything else is just the remnant of ash.

19.

You say not to bite the hand that feeds me
But how do I resist when
It's the same hand that beat me?
The weight of greed,
Bringing it down.
The weight of pride
And a false sense of respect,
Will be the very downfall of you.

I always wanted to be
In the very distant middle,
Yet you both kept dragging me
To one side or the other.
I destroy this bridge in hopes
To be light years away.
I may be of mixed emotions about it
But in my own ways I cope.
This was your doing, not mine.

I wasn't sent here from hell to be a soldier.
I was sent here to be the cause of the war.
As a punishment with the result of remorse.
A feeling where I miss my home,
There are no such things as sides for me.
Concepts like those ceased
The moment I got tossed here.

Hate is a strong word but so is love.
Both are often misused.
To label it as such would be an atrocity.
The blame game has been going on for centuries.
You live with your words as swords,
Your trust is a breach in territory
For the wrong reasons.
Why live biblically when it's like this?

I believe that biting is the way to go.

It's obvious you underestimate my ferocity.
I'm far more diabolical
Then most have led others to believe.
The problem is you're claiming to know me,
When I've left myself so concealed,
Even Satan knows not who I am.

You don't move against someone
Whose weakness is unknown to you.
Family isn't a weakness.
Loyalty and honesty didn't come overnight.
They helped me reap my strong foundation,
Emotions go off as I wish.
Moves made against me,
Need to be thought over for a long time,
Just with as much intensity if not more.

Don't try to find the link between anything and me
Or for that matter anyone.
Love, peace and kindness are hated aspects.
They let me walk through the gates of heaven,
Only to have me dropped at the Devil's doorstep.
They were the matches that lit the flame
That is now my crown.
Your efforts would only end up feeding that fire.

The darkness here can suffocate your souls.
You won't recognize me here either
So, don't search for me.
I control everything here,
Even you if you enter,
Demons won't guide you all the way through.
Even the Devil knows I own him here.

You reach the pier only to be blinded,
Everything with you both was one-sided.
I didn't want to be dragged into this rivalry.
I could only love you from a distance,
Yet you kept pushing and pulling,
Failing to realize this wasn't tug of war.

Loyalty and honesty are how it works with me
But you both faked it,
Expecting me to stick around.
You care about yourselves in the midst of my priorities.

20.

As you lie there, critical,
I'm thinking of going sinister,
With no concern for the minister.
I don't need religion,
I need the Devil himself.
Even if I take all the blowback.

I don't mind going out first.
It keeps me from handling the pain
That others leave in their tracks.
Being a few steps ahead all the time,
Is it really a crime?

Making sure that the hypocrites stay away,
The last thing anyone needs
Are their false prayers.
All they do is stab you behind your back,
Only to claim that they remember you,
As they take His name.

You don't need their God,
Nor does God need them.
I'm here defending who you are,
Knowing you don't need it.
We're brothers to the end.
So, I can't stand by and watch.

I'm saving you from every knife coming at you,
Regardless of who's holding the other end.
It's instinct I can't ignore.
It's not about push coming to shove,
It's not about having you thrown under the bus,
It's about pulling you out before any of that.
This valley belongs to me.
The shadow is one I control.

I'll let them all burn,
I can't let your recovery take a turn.
There is no compromise.
If they don't have mercy,
I'll make them beg for it.
I'll tear through their pride with my teeth,
I'll cut open their values.
Just to let them out for display.
I'll show them
Who they truly are,
Before they even dare to point at you.

I need you around.
I'll do anything to keep it that way.
You once looked out for me,
This is God's way of telling me,
I need to return the favor.
Even if I have to walk the extra ten miles,

My way is ruthless.
You should be the one left unscathed by this mess.
I fight in the most depraved manner.
You'll only have to pity them at the end.
If it's about being a ride or die,
I'll make sure the latter isn't an option.

I'll break their very will
Till they crave, still and shallow pools of blood.
I'll even baptize them in it.
I have the Devil on a leash,
Even he knows what he's been tasked with.
He won't be bought.
He knows who the highest power is-
He fears me above all else.

I'll make sure they regret
Having walked on rotten eggshells.
They were mixed with shards of glass.
This isn't revenge-

It's revival and redemption.
It's the very cleansing
Of their wayward hypocritical souls.

21.
(For those that recognize their titles more than their names)

You sit highly on a title
That holds room for replacements.
I have a disregard for you and your kind.
Sheep posing as lions,
With the brains of a pigeon.
You try to put me under pressure,
Poking me in hopes of a reaction.

You won't even let me walk in peace.
I never wanted your approach.
You want me to run out of breath.
Would my heart stopping, bring you joy?
Even though I never even glanced at you,
I want to slaughter your spirit.

I ignore vengeance and retaliation.
As you try to humiliate me,
The fire inside rages.
Parts of your very body
Would have to be found in various locations,
Unknown to the masses,
Misused authority is a spiritual crime.
You go against freedom.
You make a move against my beliefs,
The very core of my being.

I will never be honored by your presence,
I will never bow down to your orders,
I will never acknowledge your existence,
I will never give in to your threat of violence.
I can show you the most gruesome form of it,
Making you rethink your one decision
To bark at a silent Devil wolf,
Only to waste his time.

Roping him into becoming one of you,
I live for a final judgment,
Not to be shackled.
My restraint in the face of your actions, doesn't speak to you,
Even as you claim to be smart.
How could you be?
You listen to what you're told.
You're told what to believe and do.
I won't roll over like you.
I don't follow your chain of command.
I will not give in to fear,
When I'm the one that created it in this town.

22.

Your people surround me
And it only leaves me feeling like I can't breathe.
It leaves me feeling like I can't be myself,
You created me so **you** know
I'm not one to follow rules.
Your people fail to realize, they portray **you**
So, they hide their sins
As they proceed to point at mine.

They won't allow me to walk my walk.
When I falter then they talk down to me.
As if **you** didn't allow room for mistakes,
As if **you** didn't want us to learn from them,
As if **you** didn't give us free will.
The people that embody **you** here,
Only made me want to run the other way.

The Devil had no room for such things,
He gave me respect.
To be clear, **your** people
Pushed me to this.
I was on the edge,
I was barely balancing.

The world said I could do that.
The world said more and more.
I listened under an impression,
You were speaking through them.
How could they speak for **you**,
When it was only supposed to be about **you** and I?

Your people built their foundation on **you.**
Their mistake was thinking,
Their sins would be sheltered.
They forced me to own my sins
When they never looked at their own.

Your people had declared me
Fit to be **your** adversary.

I guess **your** doors aren't open for everyone.
Even the people around me
Force me to turn to **your** earthly shrine.
I saw the brutal truth from out here,
It convinced me not to ever go back inside.

Hell will be safer
Since **your** people won't be there.
That's why I call it home.
Safety means more to me
Than heaven itself if it's infested.
Safety means peace.

Your people broke me
For the sake of teaching me.
Your people slaughtered my faith.
I remain completely disoriented
At how **you** still love them
And let them personify **your** voice.

It wasn't a moment of weakness,
Nor an act of cowardice.
Being outside shed a lot of light.
The darkness was freeing
In contrast to the light **your** people
Claimed to lead me toward.

Having the ability to breathe,
Gave my mind the peace of quiet waters,
I could see my reflection…
Only to be horrified by what they had done.
I didn't run away-
I let go.

23.
(Part 2 of 22.)

You have no idea of the toll it took
To cross the bridge.
Once I did,
Everything behind me vanished,
I couldn't find my way back to **you.**
How could I, when it no longer existed?
You let them bring me to earth,
Yet **you** barely gave me time with them.

You didn't change their hearts.
One of them didn't want anything to do with me,
Because I was different?
Because I was "meant for greater things"?
Because I was bound to see the truth?
There was no room for love.
You had no idea the heartless monster
You were making.
I realized what I was
When I was thankful for being rebuked.

The other only pretended.
As I opened myself up,
You were too busy looking at the others.
You claimed to prioritize us,
But you defended him against me.
Were we really all you wanted?
I was partial when you both were mirroring each other.

You trapped me.
I never wanted to be in such deep waters,
Yet you both would storm it in a certain way
Where I couldn't save myself.
You got out of it just fine,
Creating it only to bail,
Leaving me stranded time and time again.

Why was I the odd one out?
I turned to **you**,
Yet **you** barely looked towards me.
They were **your** ambassadors doing **your** work
And it barely lasted.

It all fell down,
Leaving me caught under the weight of it all.
I could barely see it coming.
You always looked at each other,
Even making an effort to look at your favorites.
They say blood is what brings us together,
Yet it only divided me further.

When you abandoned me,
I tried to find someone I could lean on.
I was wounded,
At the tipping point of survival and death.
They only helped for a mere moment,
Only to leave me for worse,
The Devil provided a safe haven,
Whilst the flames of Hell healed me.
It was your mother that once called me the Devil.
What else could I do but own it?

Then all the eyes turned to me…
By then I was too far gone.
By then it was only time to forget who I was.
Peace turned my life into chaos.
Trust broke me,
Faith shattered me,
Loyalty stabbed me in my chest,
Love only cursed me to an eternity of misery.

Hope only buried me alive,
Kindness tore my heart out,
Patience allowed to me to persevere-
Even if it was darker.

Self-control helped me in tearing through others.
Focus and acceptance got me
To where I needed to be,
Even if it wasn't what you wanted.

24.

The rain down here is blood.
You can taste the fear and pain.
When it snows, you even learn to enjoy the red glow.
You watch as the torment melts…
The once dry rivers eventually fill up,
You hear it fill like a flood.
When it's deep enough,
You watch as the demons baptize each other,
The lakes are no longer frozen,
You can smell an atrocious spring.
When you see the movement in what were once calm waters,
You see the most fiendish creatures come out.

They pledge allegiance to me.
Their life only having one purpose.
The one I appoint to them,
They set out with their tasks,
Their hunger grows as they draw closer,
The torment they carry, ready to inflict on others,
Is used as a weapon to draw out their victims.
The one person they don't touch is *you*.

They seem to be fearless,
But the stench of their fear only grows,
When they draw nearer to me.
I appoint them with the life they momentarily enjoy.
They know I can easily wish it away,
But the limits are clear:
When they cross it, they cease to exist.
Ensuring that there are no traces of them.

This blood,
It gives life.
I will it into existence,
He gave me power over my dominion.
He knows it applies to himself as well,
Forever grateful,

Only to the victims,
They're an endless source,
As it repeats time and time again.

I set the motion here
To never result in failure,
I only monitor
When there is presence of the demons.
I fall prey to an escape
To one that draws me towards *you*.
I know it won't last.
When I remember I only aim to savor it,
I sense a trap
To have me overthrown,
I sense jealousy
When the demons figure out about my escape.

Every new day comes with new battles.
The years pass by
While I try to defend myself.
Every moment I make sure my mind is strong.
The moment I escape, I falter,
While they draw closer to the smallest hint of *you*.
Every time they consider me weak, I growl.
The weakness they think is *you*.

While in their limited knowledge,
They know not how *you* help me pull through,
They know not how *you* strengthen me,
They know not how *you* make this eternity seem like seconds,
They know not how *you* are God sent,
They know not how *you* are a full moon in this darkness,
They know not how *you* glow a light bright enough for me,
They know not how *you* guide me through this,
They know not how *you* are more than an escape.
They know not.

25.

They say a lot,
Not knowing that religion is just a word.
Religion is nothing but a pretty picture
That invokes people
To consider their life after death.
For their hearts are darker
Than the Devil with all of his darkest deeds.

Words are icing on a burning cake of coal.
They project that nothing lies within,
Chivalry is just a show
And honesty is dead.
It gives people a pass to be offensive.

People cower behind their words
In hopes that they won't be questioned.
They aspire to be something
That's not who they are.
Society has made you all mask yourselves.
You can't even be true to yourselves anymore.

You have the audacity to pull me into it.
I may be the outcast in your eyes
But for me, I cast you all out of my life.
I can't move from cage to cage,
If we all follow the law of equality,
I can't have you push me below yourselves.

I suppose thanks are in order
To myself.
If it weren't for me,
I would have never seen society for its true colors,
The society that tells me how to live my life,
That sets rules for me,
When I'm beyond perfect by doing it on my own.

I believe in me.
They want me to live the lives
They intended for themselves.
If the sky is the limit,
Is society sitting in the heavens?

I tire of their voices
So, I go to the silence,
But it's deafening.
All I can hear
Are their sayings.
I needed to get out of this damaging cycle.
Even **your** little group of people across the oceans
Are the predators in this cycle.

If they are a shadow of **your** creation,
Are **you** like them?
You claim to have created them in **your** very image.
They kill people with shame,
They set the bar using themselves.
Society and **your** people choke me,
Or at least they try to.

Society called me the Devil.
Unfortunately for them,
I became someone he tries to please.
I broke their limits
By accepting their view of me.
I am still completely myself,
I just don't credit them for this success,
For it finally silenced them.

Now their dark deeds are to be punished by me.
So, the fear stained their minds
When they dared to think about me.
They hardly uttered a whisper of my name.

26.

You thought I was subservient.
I'm not a servant.
I have a problem with authority.
I'm also fastidious.
I think they failed to mention that.
So, **you** wouldn't happen to know it
You never even cared to notice
How I turned into this.

In my mind, I see an open field.
I see *you* in all *your* beauty,
With the moon radiating it,
Away from all of them.
I walk towards *you* as I revert.
You seem to have tamed me.
I know I can be in my own skin.
I don't need to be the beast that lies within.
It doesn't inflict fear in *you*.

It shows *you,* who I used to be,
It shows *you* the cost of being me,
It shows *you* their love,
It shows *you* their fear,
It shows *you* that I was never going to heal,
It shows *you* that I would go through it all for *you*
And *you* choose to see it.

Your voice is a much-needed breeze
In my heart,
It pierces the torment I go through.
I hope *you* never meet them.
The ones responsible for this damage,
The ones who left me-
They would indeed ruin *you*.

Or ensure *you* leave me alone.

I'd try my best to shelter *you* from that,
But even Satan managed to get into the Garden of Eden.
So, what's to stop them?
They are ruthless.

I try to breathe
Because I know this moment isn't forever.
Your presence leaves a dent in my heart.
I exhale all my thoughts
In an attempt to try renewing my memories of *you*.
I want *you* to have my undivided attention,
Only *you* deserve more than that.

All of a sudden, I'm pulled out
And I'm on the run.
There's a fire in this momentary ember heart,
As I run in any direction.
I pray I run farther away from what chases me,
With a hope that has *your* name on it,
To meet without any of this behind me.

They push me over the edge,
They deprive me of my time with *you*.
There's a certain safety
In wickedness that attracts me.
It shelters me from **Your** people.
I adapted to change because of them.
In turn, I fell in love with the darkness.
I loved what it made me.
The darkness became home.

I should have been with someone,
Someone being *you*.

27.

You tell everyone you love me
But your actions tell me another story.
Always on the verge of a violent reaction
Because to you, I belong to a lower faction.
Just a solution
Because you know you never wanted me.

Not when I became such a big disappointment,
A display for everyone else to see.
When I became a damaging influence
To those around,
That's why you always tried your best
To have me done.

Once alone, always alone.
If given the chance, you'd break every bone.
Even the Holy Lord and the Devil
Look upon me with utter hate
And the scars were never shown,
But I don't know what lies ahead for my fate.
I know I'm right when I say I can't be loved.

You fall for everything outside the vase,
But where the hell are you
When every bit of torment is shoved?
You're looking at a mask.
You'd fall apart if you really saw me
And then you'd never want to pick up the pace.

PTSD from everything you did to me.
The way others could turn you against me
But you enjoyed it
And I'd end up getting hit.
Why even live
When all I am is the punching bag you take your anger out on?
When all I am and ever will be is disappointment?

A reason for torment not even in the shadows,
Which is why you were always so hell bent.
A reason for hate.
As you take your time to lure me in with the best bait,
A reason for you to turn your back on me,
Because that was the only thing you never chose to see.
A reason for you to look upon me with disgust,
Because it seemed like a must.
A reason for your disapproval,
No matter how brutal.

Me being gone to you was very crucial
And most importantly to be the cause
That rejection towards me becomes a reflex.
My soul and very being was full of defects,
Burn me at the stake,
Impale me for my make,
Shoot me for the sake of execution.
Blow me up so that I no longer have to be a problem.
For your mind or your heart or your soul.

28.
(Part 2 of 27.)

And come judgment day let me be an example,
I will be cursed.
Neither heaven overhead,
Nor hell deep below,
Neither a member of the blessed,
Nor a member of the damned.
I will be cursed to eternal pain,
Even the Lord and Devil will have something to gain.

All I ever learnt to do is embrace
And this has been an ongoing case.
Even the Devil and the Lord go against me,
Just to make you the king of everything you see,
To give you the justice you so wrongly deserve.
I wish for death the next time I'm riding on a curve.
Because every bit of my life turned out corrupt,
Until my smoothly functioning brain had been interrupted.

And I became damaged
I became dysfunctional,
I became hated,
I became rejected,
A means to an end,
I became unloved,
I became defeated,
I became hopeless,
I became loveless,
A medium of rage.

Everyone looked down on me
And turned their backs.
All they ever did was mock me.
There is no light even through the cracks,
To you I am only the bastard son,
Where it only makes me want to run,
While you take out all the fun,

Until the very day you are done.

You left me so broken.
The pieces are scattered across the oceans.
You couldn't even collect them if you tried.
But why the hell would you?
You didn't even notice when I cried.
You're a punishment from heaven and hell it's true.
You left my heart torn apart,
I can't even give it to someone
Or get a new start.
You cared about everyone else
But when it came to me you didn't even dare look.

You never listened and look where that got you?
I'm glad I got an early clue.
To you I'm nothing more than the Devil's crook.
Page after page, I write about pain,
Yet here you are…
I have to switch up my lane,
I need to leave and go someplace far.

I couldn't even notice the pain you brought onto me,
Until I bled on others.
I saw how it damaged them,
As they took a peek inside.
You'd rather team up against me
Any chance you'd get.
Like I'm a part of some debt.
You're not who you think you are.
You're the damn reason I turned into a monster.

29.

There's a certain safety in wickedness that attracts me.
A shelter from **your** people.
They are ruthless,
They are vicious.
Your people hide it all inside a clean set of clothes,
Thinking it proves they are purer,
But inside only filth is what lingers around.
They aspire to have strength in **your** name.

Respect and humility isn't strength,
Power isn't strength,
Money isn't strength.
It only invites pride and greed.
True strength stems from fear.
There is no forcing it
And it can be intoxicating,
But it helps you stay ahead.

You can ensure fear,
It's hard to maintain power and respect.
Yet people tend to go after that.
People don't go after the fear **you** instill in others,
They know it's out of their limits.
You can strike fear into the hearts of many like lightning,
The thunder that follows,
Instills the trembling in their hearts.

Evil thoughts help me sleep at night.
They are a softer pillow than caring
About people and their problems.
It keeps me guilt free and helps
Saying what needs to be said,
Doing what needs to be done,
Thinking what needs to be thought,
Hearing what needs to heard,
Showing what needs to be shown.

They say there is no rest for the wicked.
I understood that when I accepted what I was,
Then rest and peace weren't needed.
Wickedness is fulfilling.
It's a wholesome meal.
It keeps all of you away.
As I learn to bathe myself in this darkness,
It seeps into my soul,
Creating an eternal fountain inside.
The darkness flows out and then right back in.
You will get lost if you hold a gaze.
You will no longer remember who you are.
It oozes out my very words.

As I sit down to eat,
I make sure that the cries are just right.
I found them to be my favorite symphony,
I hear the darkness call out my name,
At that point, your voices just wither away.
The darkness silences all you worthless souls,
It instills peace that others find in noise.

I don't feel lonely
And I don't hide for I am one with the darkness.
The fire is the light,
A cup full of blood,
A plate with hearts,
With the fear just right.
This was a recipe that called for torment and pain.

30.

Some wounds can heal
But that doesn't mean the scar isn't there.
I can't just ignore it.
So, I keep it in mind.
Shooting stars show that they're burning.
Yet they all think it's beautiful.
So, they make wishes
Based on another's scorching.

I'm wounded and I carry it all around.
As they ask me to help them,
I lose more and more.
I never heal for they tear open my wounds
Then stab my back.

I roam with a knife protruding,
They pull it out and drive it into my chest.
You started it and people carried it on.
I hope *she* doesn't do the same
If I am ever with *her.*

I hope I don't bleed out on *her.*
I want *her* to be the moon.
There's no way I'm getting out of the darkness.
I was cursed to never see the light.
So, I hope *she* guides me with *her* faint glow.

You expect me to do so much,
While you're fixated on your priority.
You took loyalty for granted.
Never being warned about the consequences,
You were never told of what outcome beholds
Those that play with another's concern.

31.
(Part 2 of 30.)

You two pulled me to each side
And the bridge collapsed.
I went flowing with the river,
Hoping I'd drown
To put an end to all of this.
I was alive even as I fought
Instinct in my body.

I survived being caught in a flood
While the others chose and were saved.
I never wanted to be on the bridge
But you put me there,
Forcing a decision onto me.

I washed up in hell completely wounded.
The Devil used my wounds to pillar my throne.
He didn't tend to them.
He turned them into something neither of you could.
You didn't see me,
You saw a majority.

I didn't want it to be you as well
But I guess the pain never ends.
The "good" Lord has only cursed me to it.
I never tempted Eve,
She wanted to be like **you,**
Which drove her to a choice.

You punish me as if I were responsible,
Being the origin of the mayhem and slaughter.
As if I were the cause of war
Between men time and time again.
You punish me as if I'm paying the price
For the Devil and all his darkest deeds.
Will **you** have me crucified like **you** did **your** son?

You let humans send him
To a punishment he didn't deserve,
In the name of grace for humans.
They tell me to be like **your** son...
I'm no lamb, I'm a wolf.
I bare my teeth so that **you** know,
I won't waste my time barking.
I won't be nailed to a cross for the sins of the Father.
I know this pain needed to come out.
Now it is on display, near my heart.
Now people run when they see it.

Are you happy to see me?
I don't think you could be.
You never did see me,
You never did hear me.
Even as I yelled for help,
You let the water drown out my call for help.
The water even hid my tears,

You ensured I'd be in a state
Where I could no longer see *her*.
Even if *she* was meant for me,
You would tell *her* my dark deeds.
You would convince *her*
My road to redemption is non-existent.
You would make *her* turn the other way.

The Devil saw my pain, and me.
He knew the results of my state would push him out.
So, he willed into existence my own dominion.
He forged a crown.
He struck fear into the very core being of the demons-
Fear of who I am becoming.

Tell me again, are you happy?
This is the fruit of the seed you planted.
I whimpered in pain as I was sent down here.

I was already a wolf on the verge of actual death
That would ensure non-existence.

You didn't even let me have that:
One moment with *her*.
Was I to just walk as if nothing happened?
I wasn't being forced to carry a cross.
So, why is this walk weighing me down?
I'm not hard-hearted,
Since I no longer have one.

32.
(The Dream Of *You* That Woke Me Up)

Sometimes, we have the ability to do things
But we are cursed never to touch them.
Sometimes, we have the ability to meet people
But we are cursed to never be close to them.
Sometimes, we have the ability to fill ourselves with love
But we are cursed to never learn how to love.

You are the one I could never be close to.
If life allowed it,
If God allowed it,
I would have run to *you* in a single breath.
So, instead I see *you* walk past me
And I stop *you* to ask if we can talk.
So, *you* agree.
I handle other matters all the while I'm focused on *you*.

You take me to a different place.
Undivided attention,
That's the one thing I was trying to give *you*.
I had to be honest, even if it meant being slightly numb.
I gave *you* more than I could have offered to anyone.
I tried to make the most of it.
Under my breath, I just wished we'd get another chance.

The second time I came around, I didn't see *you*.
So, I sat by in patience.
After years, she came back to me.
She asked me if I did truly like *you*,
I admitted the truth.
For once I loved her as well,
She vanished just as *you* appeared.
I told *you* how she was a spark in my dark soul.
So, I understood that now
You're here to be more.

Then I woke up from that dream.

Reality hit me hard, early in the morning.
That didn't stop me from saying *your* name.
Who could I possibly talk this out with?
They would just say that I'm crazy.
If I'm crazy then why did it feel real?
Why have *you* left traces of *yourself* in my mind?
Why did it feel like I never awoke?
Why does it feel like I'm drawn to *you*?

Nature paved a path for peace to enter.
Peace of knowing that our paths would indeed cross.
I promise myself to make the most out of it,
To leave a piece of myself with *you,*
Like a pirate who hides his treasure,
My treasure too will be hidden.

The way snow piles up,
There's ice over this lake.
My heart barely beats.
It's adapted to the cold,
Yet it gets warmer with the thought of *you.*

Then I remember:
Sometimes, we're cursed, never to touch things
But that won't stop me from waiting
To see *you* walk towards me.

33.

You once said that people speak up
About the internal wounds others cause,
Yet they lie about the external ones.
I can count on cuts, bruises and stitches to heal.
My body won't fail me.
My emotions however, will.
The wounds that you cause
With words and actions,
Leave traces in the places they shouldn't,
With scars in areas, they shouldn't.

I run away from love.
I fear I will end up like one of you.
I wouldn't want that for someone else.
So, I convinced myself I'm unlovable,
The seed of wickedness settled in
And a realization that **your** book says
There's no rest for the wicked.

I broke off all that I had,
'Destroyer of lives,'
What I do is far worse than the fate of death.
Family only turned into a misused word.
Blood taught me the value of loyalty,
Blood taught me solitude,
Blood taught me to be there for myself,
Blood taught me how unfaithful it is,
Blood taught me that it dries up.
Wounds only let it all out.
Should I be glad for the lessons it left behind
With all the damage going hand in hand?

I murdered the thought of who I used to be.
We all have monsters in our heads,
But I am my monster.
I am my demon.

I am more than my own Devil.

You never let me be.
I was an adult in a child's body,
Bound to follow the timeline till I die.
I was a wolf in a human's body.
God didn't make me what I was meant to be.
He didn't want to see me free.

Society would hunt me down,
Eventually ensuring my extinction.
I was one of a kind, my own breed.
Being the first and last of my kind,
I know all I can do is walk by *you,*
When my body fights just to walk with *you.*

In this battle between body and mind,
My heart wins.
Yet it's no longer with me.
I fall through and go with the wind,
Thoughts of my ancestors surround me,
As I hear them express their despair,
I know they feel my pain.

34.

I know I will live my life behind bars.
I'm being cursed to what I love.
I'm being deprived of the one I love.
Forever to ride,
In and with the wind,
In the rain straight to the fire,
From the ice straight to the desert.

There's only one road I follow,
Leading me to hell.
I can't turn around,
I no longer decide my own fate.
I ride where the bike takes me.
This was set in motion before *you*.

You came later
When I had already paved my path,
Removing all others from the sides,
You mean more.
Life was just working against us,
That's what I tell myself…
Otherwise, I am the one to blame.
Still, I do for guilt feeds on my heart.

I know the demons impale me
That doesn't stop me from feeling
As if I am the one to be held responsible.
I never wanted this when it came to *you*.
Now they know, that pain only reminds me of *you*.
They figured out *you're* the anchor of my heart,
Emotions are a fragile deal.
Luckily mine are for *you*.

35.

The reaper called out my name.
He came to me, as I lay idle.
He then bestowed his duty upon me.
In hopes that I could meet *you* once before *you* go up,
I took on the responsibility.
Knowing very well I would forever have an obligation
To run my area of hell as well.

I would be cursed to it for eternity
Just to have a glimpse of *you*,
To share even a breath of a moment
Before our paths are forever distant.
Running in different directions,
A settlement like that is worth it
When it comes to *you*.

Your name is under my breath
Every moment I'm here.
Providing the very solace I need,
While the fire is burning bright,
The fire in my heart for *you* is brighter.
While the screams tear into my ears,
Your voice gently lays a whisper in my heart
And everything settles.

The storms in my life are many.
Yet the existence of *your* aura
Calms all of them.
I heave in hopes to get back on track,
But I know I'll need *you* more when they come back.
They say time waits for no one.
Here, time is all I have,
Hoping I can share it all with *you*.

It may not be perfect at the end
But it doesn't stop me from wanting to do it again.
The blood in my veins

Draws me to the thought of *you.*
My mind is helpless
And my heart doesn't stop.

They hail the king of the dominion.
This king rules alone.
They fear the king.
This king hopes *you* won't fear him.
He started as a slave,
Being born to a prestigious family didn't change it,
As he was forced to go from one to the other,
The tears that shed were blood.

All the while the duo of the Devil and the reaper
Watched as I grew into that,
Which they wanted.
They craved a soul like me
That was nurtured with the evil they wanted.

36.

They say there are seven princes in hell
But they don't mention me.
The worst to even be mentioned,
Born with selflessness and loyalty,
Only to end up as pure evil.
Evil was always a part of me,
Till I was one with the darkness.
The cold embrace brought out what I am.
As it woke me up,
There is sight in the darkness for me.

The road of my redemption doesn't exist,
There was but a sliver of hope
It went up in fumes to heaven,
When the heat down here burned it out.
Hope has no place here like its brothers.
Gentleness is not known here.
There is faith in pain here.
Mercy has no trace.
Still, I toil even as my breath runs out.

The Devil is my advocate.
So, how then do you plead?
The fate you will damn me to,
Will not be worse than what I've already suffered.
Fear was beaten out of me.

The horrors I've seen in my life
Created the road I was forced to ride on.
You saw to your benefit
As the blood ran down and covered old scars,
Opening them up,
Tearing them till they were deeper,
My bones now blended into the same shade.

I wonder if God makes us feel like He doesn't exist.
He caused my disbelief in His people.

His people shunned me.
They were the cause of my loss in faith.
I call **you** Father
While I sit with my brother, the Devil.
Was this the life **you** intended I live?
I was closest to **you** alone.
Your people interfered with that and I lost **you**.

Your abandonment only fostered my being,
I rode the storm.
As it harbored me in a pit of absolute darkness,
I was blinded in misery,
I was blinded in pain,
I was blinded in torment,
I was blinded in trauma,
Till the reaper gave me sight.

I tried hard to let my wounds heal.
The darkness seeped in through them,
Sneaking up and changing the very beat of my heart,
The severing of ties broke me,
Put me under significant pressure,
Turning my heart as hard as a diamond.
The hue however, stayed the same.
I gave up when I realized
The wounds will bleed forever-
They were never meant to heal.

I carry the stench of your sins.
I never wanted any part of your lives.
I always wondered why He forsook me.
You denied me my chance of reconciliation,
You pulled me into your tornado of a fight,
Spewed me out with more damage than you let on.
I am the aftermath…
The very spoils of your war.

This landscape is trapped under my paw.
The howls are silenced,

Even the birds have limits,
The mountains are buried below,
The trees are given their own shade.
You should be proud of the power I have.
Instead, you look at me as if I were a monster.
I've put everything at a standstill,
Yet you try to push me around.

Even the calmest waters wouldn't just ripple.
The waves would clash in battle with each other.
You knew no peace nor would you allow it.
I tried to silence all the aftereffects of your battles,
In my mind the echoes would ring louder and louder.

Just as they settled,
You would start another.
The middle was the center of both attacks.
The distance was what I tried to run towards.
Anywhere farther away from your war zone.
I don't see a border,
I only see casualties,
Shards of my soul lying all around
Wasn't incentive enough for you to halt.

You ignore all the fruits of your vicious seeds.
They bare a poison that won't even allow a glimpse.
You were proud if I were to stumble
And do something good.
Even if it had nothing to do with you,
I was embarrassed by good deeds.
It gave people a false impression of who I was.

I never needed those high and low tides,
When tidal waves were already headed my way.
I was trying to stay up,
Then your whirlpool sucked me in.
I drowned over and over again,
Forever surviving.
That's why the wounds never turn to scars.

37.

This darkness may be my eternal damnation,
But I've come to terms with that fate.
I wandered by *you*
While being tossed around,
Lost with no desire for being found.
A whiff of *your* essence is all it took
To try and break these shackles
To try healing,
To try to be noticed,
To try to be worth… *you*.

It gets harder
To convince myself to be numb
When *you're* already inside,
Trying to shatter the solidity
That took decades to build.
With pain that dried up,
Wounds were now empty,
Scars gave up hiding
And desolation became me.

The slaughter of who I used to be
Was an unhurried agony,
It creeps up on me.
Reminding me of my horrors,
Nostalgia of the pain I endured,
Memories that burn my brain.
As the heat singes my heart,
Moments of peace are long forgotten,
With unknown times of a past ignored.

I am yet to weigh in
On whether *you* are for amusement
Of the ones who seek my downfall
Or if *you* really are there.
Not just some mendacious plight

For an increase in commitment.
They want me to finish things,
They detest a certain intention
Of *you* having a place in this turmoil of a life.
There is a basis for their detest.

They tell me to avoid conduits of momentary peace,
Though that is all I have
In this world that's forever chaotic.
They call them addictions and bondages,
Yet they are the ones that use them
To hold onto me
And put me under the weight of their pride.
I envision a peace
Embodied by *you*.

They want me to be one of them,
As they chase each other's tails.
I exist beyond that.
The one they praised, cursed me
To such a vision of this life.
Their prayers create a certain misgiving
I can go on without them, not *you.*
I was better off when they weren't uttered for me.
Words do more harm than swords and guns.
They are the incentive for pain and havoc.

They never see the shattered soul within
That they mobbed against to demolish.
They judge the shackles
As they murder all that lies within-
All that *you* resurrected.

38.

I wear bullets on my neck
To memorialize the violence of others.
It knows no bounds.
I'm here for me and I'm here for *you*,
The rest are roadkill.
The rest are not my concern.

I had once put them first
And they left me for dead.
They were caught up with themselves,
Leaving me to fend for myself.
They were caught up with greed,
Leaving me buried under its weight.
As I opened the doors for them,
They forced me out of my own home.

One reminds me of the time the institutes failed.
The time I taught myself,
In three years of struggle,
With failure after failure.
It tends to happen when you're cast out,
Thrown down from a pedestal,
Immediate change wasn't facile.

It left no room for misplaced steps,
As the ones watching over me
Held high expectations,
When I was trying to figure myself out.
They held high demands,
As if I were living for them.

The other reminds me
Of my mornings in nature's peace,
Where I convinced myself, *you* were
Sitting beside me.
Even if the moments were brief,
Just us, with two of my furry brothers.

I wish I could take *you* there.
A world away from their clutches
To be blessed by nature with all it has to offer.

They wanted to be my moral compass-
I never let them.
I was never grounded
What would I ever need them for?
I never wanted to be caged.
I saw as they had laid out their snare,
I never wanted to be shackled,
I saw as they forged chains for me.

I flew higher out of their sight
But I couldn't fly forever.
I needed to land someplace.
You have always been in my sight,
Even if it was just in concept.

They were just sheep
That made a grave mistake.
They were sheep that were foolish
To think they belonged alongside a wolf.
They never appreciated the hunt,
They couldn't handle the glorious smell of blood,
They couldn't color themselves with it,
They had no viciousness,
They couldn't keep up.

They believed that **you** would turn me into one of them.
They had no idea **you're** the reason I am the wolf,
They thought I faltered in my path.
Failing to grasp my sense of adventure,
I sat at places high in elevation,
As they feared death
I stood at its precipice.
They fell one by one,
As I pushed them over.
Life with fear is a life not lived.

39.

I'm one of the ferocious few.
Only one of them.
I fear others may not live up to me.
Forsaken with this trauma,
Forsaken with this pain,
Forsaken with this hard heart,
Forsaken on this path.

You always labeled me as such.
The one before you called me the Devil.
I had to live up to something,
Even if it was this unholy.

My heart knows this was where I was headed.
It has learnt to accept all of it.
I wonder why all of you leave me forlorn.
Was it retribution?
It tore my heart
I felt it as the wounds stretched and ripped.
I feel it even more now.

It only taught me
I am for myself.
Your retribution foreshadowed my vigor,
This road is narrow
But you knew that.
I had to flit without *you*.
You alleviated the consequences by burning the ties,
Now these tears foster a hurricane,
As I persuade myself that this was bound to happen.

You turned into the one you hated.
The one whose deeds you replicate.
I condemn myself because
I should have discerned earlier.
I look at this blade perturbing.
I can barely reach for it

I see more all around my spine
But I fail to see you.
These memories aim for it at my heart.

These wounds never heal,
They petrify my heart.
You may be afar,
But the effects of your doing
Created souvenirs in my mind,
Which torment me.
The darkness surrounded me
And you were no longer in sight.

The consolation set in
That nothing lasts endlessly.
I had to pick up where you left off.
Sculpting myself in the manner you started.
I may be a horrid beast
But I remember how I embraced
This direction you set me on.

You may get me on my knees
But my head will never turn down.
You expose your fear
I've been indoctrinated to exploit it.
I was edified to visualize your mind as a mine,
Digging deeper and deeper,
Burrowing till I find value
In a memory or weakness.

The darkness sought comfort in me.
So, it resides there.
I learnt to master it.
I own it now.
Acceptance was the match,
Lighting this everlasting ember.

40.

The moon knows *your* name,
It's at her very core.
She may never tell *you*
All that I have shared with her.
She sees my passion,
Yet she wants me to try on my own.
So, this wolf stands in her light,
In hopes of being in *your* presence.

I'm the wolf that never puts his head down,
Yet I do so for *you*.
I'm the wolf that never put others first,
Yet I do so for *you*.
I'm the wolf that never dreamt,
Yet I do dream of *you*.

The trees know *your* name.
It's engraved in their roots,
The air they let out, has traces of *you*.
While people may not know it,
The roots bring out a version of *you*.
So, I go following *you* into the woods.

I'm searching for *you* in her.
This emptiness is what draws me to *you*.
You reveal a unique beauty to me.
One that has shaped me.
My time with *you* is limited.
So, I make the most while I can.

You're the secret I share with nature,
Never to be known by man.
Your name remains known
By everything here.
Let me be buried here,
I'll be around my thoughts of *you*.

41.

You're the moon in my life,
I look for *you* every night.
I rarely see *you* completely,
I cherish those moments when I do,
Making the most of it as long as it lasts,
Wishing it to go on forever,
Part of *you* isn't merely enough.
I appreciate the crescent,
But I crave the light *you* disperse
When *you* shine completely.

The stars amplify *your* magnificence,
Even the ones that pass by.
The galaxies are merely a reflection of *your* eyes.
I use this as an attempt
To convey *your* impact,
From a distance,
Larger than me,
Brighter than me.
Yet just enough to mean everything to me.

Holding everything together,
You keep the low tides
When the darkness crashes over me.
You bring the high tide
When *you* feel me getting closer to the edge
So, I don't fall on the rocks.

You expose the beauty of this vista.
The light may be unique,
It still shines over.
Sufficient for my eyes,
I look over to the sky for I am drawn to *you.*
Every night, whether *you* are there or not,
I talk to the stars about *you* in your absence,
Wishing to shooting stars *you* come back sooner.

When *you* are there,
I take in the beauty while I can.
I take in the light while I can.
I whisper to *you,*
Knowing full well *you* can't hear me.
That doesn't stop hope.
That doesn't stop faith.
It doesn't stop commitment.

You put a vision in my eyes.
I still wish *you* were here with me.
You make the darkness a fascinating habitat.
For it is here I see *you.*
For it is here *you* expose extravagance.
It's here where I begin to heal.
It's here where I begin to feel.

The darkness fails to catch on
How *you* empower me,
How *you* give me resilience,
How *you* became a reason,
A reason to go on.
A purpose
To one day be by *your* side.
Whether it take a night or an eternity.

42.
PART 2
{The Devil, The Demons, and The Storm}

I see the night sky overcast.
Your light is blocked.
I thought this was a reflection of my grief,
However, I accept nature's course.
As he shows me the eye of the storm,
I see distant waters tremble,
I feel the earth shake.

I reckon if I can get through it,
As I determine the impact it'll have on me.
If I will value *you* after,
Or if I will have to rebuild out of fragments.
I try to prepare
To withstand this storm
So, it does no alteration.

I see the riders on the storm.
The demons are here to pour down their wrath,
They have the stench of malice,
The scent grows stronger,
They have revenge on their tongues.
I hear it as it encroaches.
The storm fails to drown it out.

I hold my ground alone.
Opposed by a legion,
Even he leaves.
He knows well their motive.
He knows my grit,
He's shrewd enough to remain impartial.

He fears my silence.
The distress it causes seeps inside him.
He fears my scars.
They ran deep in front of him,

He fears my wounds.
I still fight on with them.

He fears the pain I endure.
He knows I'm fighting for more.
He fears the darkness inside,
For it wasn't wrought in by him,
He fears my nerve,
He knows how it got me here.

He advised the demons
Against such irrationality.
They stood by this mutiny.
I will not cower because
They blemished my time with *you*.
Silence is no longer an option.
I'm the unholiest here.
They stampede into their own demise.

It's finally touched the shore.
Trees begin to tear off their roots.
The sand flying,
Fails to impair my sight.
They've reached the threshold.
I open my arms to the destruction,
I open my arms to the devastation.

43.

My spirit is more defiant-
More than I am led to believe.
I know not to test its limits,
Yet while I stay quiet,
They keep barking,
As they threaten to bite,
They rattle the beast's cage.

They call it horrid,
They fail to see it's who I am.
These chains disappear,
For they decide when I shall battle.
They undermine my blatant disregard
For their lives.
So, my brothers let me punish them.

These shackles are let back on
When the deed is done.
When they see my teeth colored with blood,
I've painted a picture of terror
With them as my canvas and paint.
They admire my artistry.

It's only an expression
That I had to let out.
I once tried to control it
Only to end up harming myself,
Feeling what I had done to others,
These shackles cut my skin.
They broke my bones
Still, I didn't cease my attempt to break free.

I walk beside death.
It dares not touch me.
I wait for it to take me.
Still, it only hovers around.
I walk towards it,

Yet only to repel it further.

Death becomes my shadow,
Lingering ahead or behind.
Lingering faintly,
I try to fall back so I am one.
One with death,
Yet I still remain.
Tell me, am I no longer fit for death?

44.
(Burning Bridges)

Do I burn these bridges?
Because I want to build stronger ones
I can stand on.
Something without the fear of falling,
Something to bring about assurance.

Do I burn these bridges?
Because I want them to be made more permanent.
People fall through,
They prove to never be there,
They change with the wind.

Do I burn these bridges?
Because I want to.
These people brought nothing on me,
My time had been wasted.
Or, is it because I believe
Only I am there for me?

Do I burn these bridges?
Because they don't resonate with me.
I don't see my reflection in the water below,
I fail to ensure my side was made mine,
These people never stood for me.

Do I burn these bridges?
So, I can see a Phoenix rise out of the ashes,
In hopes to make way for the new?
In hopes for a new creation
To let in more?

Do I burn these bridges
To keep myself warm?
For they made me cold,
I see the water frozen below,
Stuck in the same place it was years ago.

I fear my life will end up the same.

Do I burn these bridges
To watch the flames dance?
For it resembles an art.
It resembles poetry,
Showing a hidden passion.
Or, do the flames give hope?

Why do I burn these bridges?
I will never know.
With so many there,
I plead and walk over the ashes.
Do I do it so I don't walk over blood?
Or is it about burning them?
So as to enjoy smoke.

45.

I'm not exactly following the crowd...
Not of earth anyway.
In hell, I have a crowd at my tail.
The reaper stays close behind
With his scythe at my throat,
How long I have left here,
Bothers me not.

I made memories,
I made my life.
I was prepared to go.
Many moons have passed since
His henchmen would surround me,
Assigning me my duty,
While they were assigned to inflict pain.

I was soldiered to ruin it all,
For everything around me
My touch was made to unravel,
To create chaos,
To turn sparks into fires,
To watch fights turn to wars,
To turn a needle into a sword.

I watch life turn to death.
Is it a curse?
I want to watch my end as well.
A world with pain causes more,
A world with chaos turns into agony,
A world with war turns to loss.

I wonder if I entered this earth
At the wrong time.
Would it have changed anything?
Considering my fate,
Would it change anything?
Considering my curse...

I hadn't realized I was being recruited,
Rising above the ranks
To create a rank of my own.
Revered or feared among them,
This was an unconscious success.
This effort was aimed for something else.

I had freedom.
I gave it up for a deal.
I offered myself.
I had nothing to take,
Only everything to give.
Maybe my bargain was my mistake.

46.

Your voice matches that of the angels in heaven
Maybe even more so.
My ears rarely grasp *your* tune
For I am not yet used to it.

You belong in heaven,
I knew it when I saw *you*.
I wonder why *you* ended up here.
Does God falter
Or does he show me that, which I can never have?

You seem to be the destination
But this journey seems endless.
Still, I go on regardless.
I caught myself feeling for *you,*
Knowing not even a hint of *you,*
Wondering of the possibility,
Hoping there is a why.

My devotion was for the greatest of things-
You seem to be more.
I remain conflicted between want and need,
Confused as to where *you* lay,
I can't rest anything on a maybe-
Not when it comes to *you*.

You may not want to be here
But *you've* already left *your* mark.
I don't see things turning back,
You remain irremovable.
Everything seems to be rooting itself deeper.

47.
(A Sinner's Honesty)

They go in all their own corners
To follow through with their disgraceful deeds.
We all do.
I was one to admit,
Leaving them baffled.

Honesty was meant to be the right policy.
Yet, why do I get shamed for it?
I blew open the corner,
To breathe in the fresh air.
You say He sees everything
So, why do you hide?

Out in the open,
Where he can be juror,
As he waits to discern
Whether or not I stay here,
He respects the display.
I feel freedom more than I was led to believe.

I fail to live for their opinions.
Out in the open was made for me.
Not behind locked doors,
Not behind covered windows,
Not buried under the ground,
Not within the heart.

Their judgments fail to impact me.
I would say I was cut from a different cloth,
But excess diamond was cut off me.
My heart was made harder.
This heart is a stone everyone seems to want,
But they fail to see the consequences
That comes with the solidity.

48.

I fear this black rainbow-
More what may reside on the other side.
The demons I will encounter,
This rainbow sprouted from my throne
From the blood that was shed.

Things seem to go from worse to worst.
Will it ever stop?
Every time I think I've reached the climax,
I see myself at the bottom.
This everlasting climb-
It keeps me heaving.

This suffering is infinite.
I know it by the way it feels,
Days go by but nothing changes.
So, I guess times don't change.
I do with this time what I want.

It once gripped me with fear.
It held my throat.
So, as to never speak,
It blocked my mind.
So, as to never turn to action,
It blocked my heart.
So, as to never write.

I make a cross
As I stub it out.
While the ashes are still burning,
It's become a ritual
To keep them away.
So, *you* don't get caught in the crossfire.

49.

I wish the darkness were scattered,
Not the pain.
It spreads like a wildfire,
The darkness would have been in bits everywhere.
Instead of the pain growing,
Creating its home in my heart,
While my home was long gone and vanished.
It won't even let me see *you* as home.

I wish the pain were scattered,
Not the darkness.
It left everything drowned underneath.
Pain would be easier to heal
If it were about doing so one by one.
It devoured my heart,
Replacing my sense of home,
Depriving me of being worthy of it.
It knew *you* would come along.

Pain is smarter,
Darkness is dominating,
Pain created my future,
Darkness covered my movement,
Pain barely left me breathing,
Darkness quenched my thirst,
Pain prepared a table,
Darkness only ushered in more pain.

I wish I could feed off of pain-
Not the darkness.
Yet all I have is fear.
The darkness devoured all sentiment,
The darkness makes it intimate.
I don't want to know them,
I want to know *you*.
Without all the allure of this endless shadow.

I wish I could feed off of darkness-
Not the pain.
It only brings back more,
The pain wounds me further
The pain stiffens my heart,
I want to open it up for *you,*
But I know it'll let out a river of blood
And I don't want to bleed on *you.*
I want to leave a remnant
Even if it isn't enough,
In hopes that a little goes a long way.

I have no earthly idea if *you* would read this,
I pay my dues to honesty in advance.
So that this time may be different,
I try to reach out.
It doesn't seem like I could do more.
I know I could.
I'm being pulled in opposing directions,
A deal of the past that grips my soul
And *your* presence in my heart.

Pain and darkness fight inside,
They leave a battlefield,
One I don't want *you* to witness.
I never would tell *you* the least
About what I am.
I don't think *you'd* ever remain the same.
Such devastation is never to be directed towards *you*
When *you* have *your* own halo as a Deity.

50.

Over here, beware of your shadow.
It tells me more than your words.
It leaves whiffs
Of the places you've been.
It carries the past that follows you.

My past has led me here,
My shadow is deceptive
It remains cryptic,
I've been holding on for so long,
When too much has already gone wrong
But I don't let that stop me.

I fight this darkness
For what I feel,
Knowing it is truth.
Even while I bleed out,
Time doesn't change that,
It only matures it.

This place restricts similar thoughts
To the ones I have of *you*.
Yet here I own this Hell.
I do as I please.
So, I surround myself with them.
It ensures safety in me.

You are the very heavenly light
In this hellish darkness,
Making my commitment stronger
To crawl out of here,
No matter how it disfigures me.

My shadow remains unaware
Of what goes on inside.
It protects those that plot
From in front,

To hold the knives back.
Even as they find their way through,
It keeps *you* safe
From the pain I suffer.
Let me go down as a martyr.

51.

A missed opportunity,
Is a life not lived
When it comes to *you.*
I write these words
To take a shot in the dark,
Following wherever it leads me,
Be it an abyss or a cloud.

They talk about the words not said.
So, I wrote this for *you,*
In hope to set something in motion.
Regret tends to do more damage than guilt.
I consider which one I'd rather live with.

I don't want the life of want,
I look at what I need.
Wants can be put aside
Needs are what life revolves around.
As the moon,
Everything in my life balances around *you.*

I don't want the life of unfulfilled wishes,
Where everything remains not acted upon.
Actions remain thoughts,
Where words are spoken under breaths
That barely seem to come out.
Where wishes are consumed by cowardice
That seems to have fruition.

I don't want this tree to be judged
Because there were a few bad apples.
For the tree still bears fruit,
For the tree is still beautiful
For the tree still has use.

This idea of paradise was troublesome in disguise.
My eyes aren't set on *you.*

My heart is.
My eyes can waver all they want,
It doesn't stop my heart
From being where it should be
With *you*.

Appreciation isn't merely enough
For the thought of *you*.

[This Is For The One This Book Was Made For]

You were the artists
That painted my heart, soul and life black.
Coloring it with a darkness that blinded others.
It was something I was forced to live with,
Since there was no light around me.
Then **you** dared to send missionaries my way,
Knowing full well the outcome would be gruesome.

I don't even have skeletons in the closet.
I have dead bodies and the Devil himself.
Many thought my closet to be hell,
Another bunch thought it to be a gateway there.
I never asked to be this way until you forced me to.
I let you have that brief moment of power over me,
Only for me to come out on top.
It may be foul play
But nothing you did was fair either.

A few moments in paradise
And you denied me my peace.
Then you proceeded to yours
At the cost of the destruction of mine.
You leapt into the arms of yours
As if I had done that to you.
Forever framed of the wrong you did to me.

I was convinced such a pleasure was not mine to have-
Not in this lifetime.
Not with all this coming at me from close behind,
It would be a wasted effort to involve *you,*
Only to shelter *you*
Then have *you* broken.
I'm damaged and I'd leave *you* just the same.
So, I steer by *you*
As I try and hide these tears of blood that come out.

I want to have *you* by my side at any given moment.
If I can be with *you* and breathe at the same time,
As if nothing were to happen,
As if they wouldn't show up disguised as fate,
They appear as more of a curse.
As they lead me to believe that I am safe,
I would be if I were with *you*.

So, here I sit,
Looking at the city below me in the distance,
While I wish *you* were here.
I conjure *you* up in my subconscious
And I talk as if *you* were actually here,
Pouring my heart out to *you*.

The emotions others can't believe I have,
I exhibit in front of *you*.
Even if *you* may not actually be there with me,
It's as comforting as a fire.
In this snowstorm that happens to be my life,
It's the only thing that keeps me sane.
In a certain way, I appreciate *your* existence
Even if *you're* not there with me.

This isn't about a beauty and a beast.
You're beyond beautiful.
Words will never do *you* any justice.
As for me, I'm more than any beast.
I'm hellish.
I'm monstrous and horrific in sight.

I'm wounded,
I'm scarred,
I'm barely keeping alive,
I'm hunted.
I'm choosing to persevere,
For it is those glimpses of *you* that give me purpose.
It's almost as if in some way
You drag me away and I no longer live with any of it.

Then reality hits me.
To say that Hell burns me would be apt.
I look at my crown,
The crown that identifies me.
I look at my scars,
The scars that made the foundation of my throne.
I look at my wounds,
The wounds that never seemed to heal-
Until *you* were momentarily there.

I look at the remnants of the blood of my victims,
The victims I rule over.
I look at my kingdom
That reeks with the fear of the demons-
A scent I've grown familiar with.

I realize that *you're* a distant memory.
One that I prefer to go to as an escape,
Hoping that escape lasts forever.
I realize *you're* a dream.
One that will barely come true.
Yet I find myself ready to bet on, barely.
I realize *you're* a person
I'm willing to make any and every sacrifice for
One that I wouldn't mind repeating,
In horrible variations that I would receive with open arms.

I realized, *you're* an extravagant soul
My heart belongs with.
Even if it means I can't ever be with *you*.
I'd ensure my heart would indeed be bound
With the image and thought of *you*-
Even if there is a light trace.

This isn't what they wanted me to be.
I never did what others wanted.
This isn't the path their God chose for me to follow.
I never really did hear him when I needed it.
This isn't whom I was set out to be.
I'm glad it opened my eyes to *your* existence.

This isn't pretty or anything of the sort.
This is what I am (unfortunately without *you*, this is what I am…)

AFTERWARD

This poetry book has an order known to the author alone. It has a certain flow of emotions and conflict rooted inside. I hope at least one of my readers relates to or understands it.

THE LAST POEM WAS WRITTEN BEFORE MANY OF THE OTHERS. IT'S FOR SOMEONE I FEEL DIFFERENTLY FOR COMPARED TO OTHERS THAT CAME BEFORE. AFTER A CERTAIN POINT THIS BOOK FOLLOWS CERTAIN POSITIVITY OR LIGHT, AND THAT HAPPENED WHEN I FIGURED OUT WHO SHE WAS.

Made in the USA
Las Vegas, NV
20 July 2021